INDIAN TRAILS
PUBLIC LIBRARY DISTRICT
WHEELING, ILLINOIS 60090
847-459-4100

The **Ohio** River

by Tom Jackson

Gareth Stevens Publishing
A WORLD ALMANAC EDUCATION GROUP COMPANY

Please visit our web site at: www.garethstevens.com
For a free color catalog describing Gareth Stevens Publishing's list of high-quality
books and multimedia programs, call 1-800-542-2595 (USA) or 1-800-387-3178
(Canada). Gareth Stevens Publishing's fax: (414) 332-3567.

Library of Congress Cataloging-in-Publication Data

Jackson, Tom, 1953–
    The Ohio River / by Tom Jackson.
       p. cm. — (Rivers of North America)
    Includes bibliographical references and index.
    Contents: An all-American river—From source to mouth—The life of the river—
A route to the West—Center of industry—Places to visit—How rivers form.
    ISBN 0-8368-3759-2 (lib. bdg.)
    1. Ohio River—Juvenile literature. [1. Ohio River.] I. Title. II. Series.
  F516.J33   2003
  977—dc21   2003042797

This North American edition first published in 2004 by
Gareth Stevens Publishing
A World Almanac Education Group Company
330 West Olive Street, Suite 100
Milwaukee, Wisconsin 53212 USA

Original copyright © 2004 The Brown Reference Group plc. This U.S. edition copyright © 2004
by Gareth Stevens, Inc.

Author: Tom Jackson
Editor: Tom Jackson
Consultant: Judy Wheatley Maben, Education Director, Water Education Foundation
Designer: Steve Wilson
Cartographer: Mark Walker
Picture Researcher: Clare Newman
Indexer: Kay Ollerenshaw
Managing Editor: Bridget Giles
Art Director: Dave Goodman

Gareth Stevens Editor: Betsy Rasmussen
Gareth Stevens Designer: Melissa Valuch

Picture Credits: Cover: The Point, Pittsburgh, Pennsylvania. (Skyscan: Aerials Anywhere)
Contents: Coal barge on the Ohio River.

Key: l–left, r–right, t–top, b–bottom.
Ardea: Ken Lucas 11b; Bethlehem Steel: 24; Corbis: 18, 21; Bettmann 5t, 19, 23, 29t; Richard A. Cooke 14;
Richard Hamilton Smith 9b; Dave G. Houser 27; Bob Krist 28; David Muench 7; D. Robert & Lorri Franz
12b; Charles E. Rotkin 5b, 13t, 20; Joseph Sohm/ChromoSohm Inc. 29b; Getty Images: 15, 16/17; Greater
Cincinnati Conventions & Visitors Bureau: 26; Gregory Thorp: 25t; Kentucky Department of Travel: 25b;
ORSANCO: 13b; PhotoDisc: C. Borland/Photolink 4/5; Topham: 8/9; U.S. Army Corps of Engineers: 22;
West Virginia Division of Tourism: 6, 10, 11t, 12t

Printed in the United States of America

1 2 3 4 5 6 7 8 9 07 06 05 04 03

Table of Contents

An All-American River

Hundreds of years ago, settlers traveled down the Ohio River in search of new lives. Today, almost one in ten Americans lives in the region, which has become an important center of industry.

The Ohio River got its name from the Iroquois word for "beautiful water." This great river flows from the Allegheny Mountains of West Virginia and Pennsylvania to the Mississippi River.

The Ohio River was an important route taken by pioneers and settlers heading west, and control of it was fought over for many years. Today, the river flows past some of the country's major centers of industry, where tons of steel, glass, and coal are produced. It carries more cargo than any other U.S. river except the mighty Mississippi.

Fighting for Control

By the early 1600s, after European settlers arrived in North America, the Iroquois Confederacy moved into the area and began to sell furs to European traders. A few years later, the French and British armies

The Ohio River begins in the center of Pittsburgh, where two smaller rivers flow into one another.

were at war over the land, and the banks of the Ohio had become a battleground.

Center of Industry

The Ohio River of today is still at the center of American life. The Ohio forms the borders of five states: Illinois, Indiana, Kentucky, West Virginia, and Ohio. The river flows through a heavily populated area of the United States, moving past several large cities, including Louisville, Kentucky; Cincinnati, Ohio; and Pittsburgh, Pennsylvania. Outside of the cities, the Ohio River Basin has mines that produce coal, salt, and stone. The river also passes through farmland, where soybeans, tobacco, and corn are grown.

Left: *A family of settlers steers its flatboat down the Ohio River in the seventeenth century, carrying all their belongings with them.*

Below: *Huge barges carry food, raw materials, and factory-made products along the Ohio. These barges can travel as far as the Gulf of Mexico, by way of the Mississippi River.*

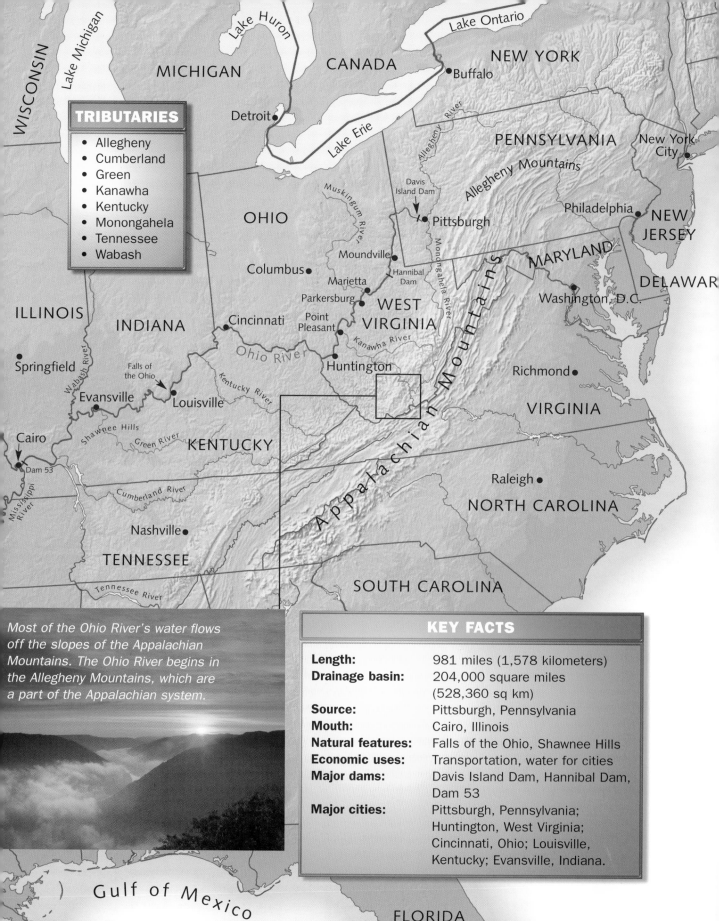

TRIBUTARIES

- Allegheny
- Cumberland
- Green
- Kanawha
- Kentucky
- Monongahela
- Tennessee
- Wabash

Most of the Ohio River's water flows off the slopes of the Appalachian Mountains. The Ohio River begins in the Allegheny Mountains, which are a part of the Appalachian system.

KEY FACTS

Length:	981 miles (1,578 kilometers)
Drainage basin:	204,000 square miles (528,360 sq km)
Source:	Pittsburgh, Pennsylvania
Mouth:	Cairo, Illinois
Natural features:	Falls of the Ohio, Shawnee Hills
Economic uses:	Transportation, water for cities
Major dams:	Davis Island Dam, Hannibal Dam, Dam 53
Major cities:	Pittsburgh, Pennsylvania; Huntington, West Virginia; Cincinnati, Ohio; Louisville, Kentucky; Evansville, Indiana.

From Source to Mouth 1

The Ohio River and its tributaries collect most of the water draining from the west side of the Appalachian Mountains. The river flows from Pennsylvania to the Mississippi River.

The Ohio River collects water from 204,000 square miles (528,360 sq km) of land in a total of nine states, from New York to Alabama. The river is 981 miles (1,578 km) long, and most of it is about 24 feet (7 meters) deep.

The Ohio River begins at The Point in the center of the city of Pittsburgh, Pennsylvania, where the Monongahela and Allegheny Rivers flow into one another. The Allegheny begins in the high country of northern Pennsylvania. It flows for 325 miles (523 km) before joining the Monongahela. The Monongahela River flows 128 miles (206 km) from the mountains of West Virginia into Pennsylvania.

Above: *The Allegheny River winds through the hills of Pennsylvania. The river took its present course ten thousand years ago, after glaciers melted away.*

East to West

From Pittsburgh, the Ohio River flows across a flat area of land called the Appalachian Plateau. The Appalachian Plateau extends from New York state all the way to Alabama. The northern section of the plateau was flattened into low, rolling

PARKS AND FORESTS

- Blennerhassett Island, West Virginia
- Great Serpent Mound, Hillsboro, Ohio
- Hoosier National Forest, Indiana
- Shawnee National Forest, Indiana
- Wayne National Forest, Ohio

hills by glaciers during ice ages in the past 100,000 years. Farther south, the plateau is covered by rugged hills and valleys. At its mouth, the Ohio releases 2 million gallons (7.6 million liters) of water every second into the Mississippi River. The Mississippi only becomes the largest river in the United States after the Ohio has emptied into it.

Through the Hills

Forming the border between West Virginia and Ohio, the Ohio River passes through the northern part of the Appalachian Plateau. Here, the river winds around low hills. This part of the river's course cuts through the main coal-producing area in the United States.

Near Parkersburg, West Virginia, Blennerhassett, a long, thin island, appears in the river. From here, the Ohio moves south into the more rugged area of the Appalachian Plateau. The riverbanks are much steeper along this stretch of the river. The river's course twists and turns as it heads toward Kentucky.

The Ohio River then flows west away from the hills and heads toward Cincinnati, Ohio, one of its major ports. Here, the river is straddled by the world-famous Bluegrass region. This area of rolling hills gets its name from the tiny blue flowers

Below: *The Ohio River flows through low, forested hills in Kentucky.*

that appear on grass plants each May, coloring the land for a few short weeks.

Falls of the Ohio

From Cincinnati, the Ohio River swings toward the southwest and flows along the southern border of Indiana. At Louisville, Kentucky, the Ohio drops 24 feet (7 m) in 2.25 miles (3.6 km), forming the largest rapids on the river. The rapids are called the Falls of the Ohio. (A canal has now been built around the Falls of the Ohio.) Past the port of Louisville, Kentucky, the Ohio River once again flows through an area of rugged land, called the Shawnee Hills. Beyond the Shawnee Hills, the Wabash River flows into the Ohio and marks the three-state boundary of Indiana, Kentucky, and Illinois.

The Ohio River is met by two more rivers before it runs its course. Both of these tributaries—the Tennessee River and Cumberland River—drain water from the south and join the Ohio a few miles from its mouth.

The Ohio ends at Fort Defiance near Cairo, Illinois, where it empties into the Mississippi River. Cairo got its name from the capital city of Egypt, because the confluence of the two rivers looks similar to the Nile River Delta in Egypt.

The Mississippi River flows under a bridge before meeting the Ohio. At this point, the Ohio River is carrying more water than the Mississippi.

2 The Life of the River

The wealth of wildlife along the Ohio River is what first attracted settlers to the area. Over the years, however, pollution made by people has had a damaging effect on the plants and animals.

The Ohio River flows more or less from east to west, and its source is just a few hundred miles (km) north of its mouth. Therefore, places along the river have similar weather. It is slightly wetter and colder in places around the headwaters of the river and warmer and drier in places near its mouth. Most places get about 60 inches (152 centimeters) of rain per year. In winter, it rarely gets much below freezing (32°F; 0°C), while in the summer, the temperature is regularly above 80°F (27°C).

Above: *Canada geese swimming in a quiet place on the Ohio River. These birds stop at the river during their long journey north in summer.*

Forest and Grass

Forests grow along the banks of eastern sections of the Ohio River, especially in the mountainous regions. In the west, the forests give way to open grasslands in places. The forests along the river are filled with beech, hickory, maple, and sycamore trees. Smaller plants include shrubs, such as dogwood and hawthorn.

Many animals live among the trees and grasses along the riverbanks, including white-tailed deer, raccoon, chipmunks, opossums, and groundhogs. Animals such

Right: *A blue heron watches for prey in shallow water. It uses its long, sharp beak to grab fish and frogs.*

BIG MUSKY—KING OF THE OHIO RIVER

The muskellunge (below) is a large river fish common in the waters of the Ohio River. The muskellunge is also known as the "musky" and is the world's largest type of pike. Some muskies reach 6 feet (1.8 m) long and weigh almost 100 pounds (45 kilograms), but most are about half this size. Muskies can live up to twenty-five years.

Like other pike, muskellunges are hunters. They will eat almost anything, but they prefer small fish. They are very aggressive and will often fight each other.

Muskies are highly prized by fishers because they are difficult to catch. Once caught, many are displayed as trophies, but their meat is also good to eat.

Muskrat themselves are at risk from attack by hunters, such as hawks and coyotes. Mink are another enemy of muskrat. The two animals are often close neighbors on the riverbank. Mink are relatives of weasels, which hunt both on land and in water. As well as muskrat, mink eat frogs and small fish. Unlike muskrat, mink cannot see very well under water. They stay on land and watch the water for prey, before diving in for the kill.

Left: A young white-tailed deer watches out for danger in a grassy meadow. These deer live in most wild places along the Ohio River.

as beavers, muskrat, and mink live beside the river and its tributaries. Muskrat are small burrowing rodents that make their homes in tunnels dug into riverbanks. They feed on river plants, such as bulrushes and cattails. When they find them, muskrat will also feast on crayfish, clams, and snails.

Fur Animals

Muskrat and mink have thick, sleek fur. Traders were among the first Europeans to travel down the Ohio River, attracted by the rich supply of furry animals. Fur was one way people kept warm before modern fabrics were invented. Muskrat and mink furs are

Below: A mink stands on the riverbank and keeps a lookout for prey in the water. Its thick fur coat keeps the animal warm underwater.

KEEPING THE RIVER CLEAN

The Ohio River provides drinking water for more than three million people, but the river's water carries pollution (waste products). This pollution comes from the area's factories, farms, and cities. The Ohio River Valley Water Sanitation Commission (ORSANCO) makes sure that the water in the Ohio River is clean enough for people to use.

ORSANCO was set up more than fifty years ago. Its scientists regularly test samples of water taken from the Ohio River and its many tributaries. High school students often help with this big job. If high levels of pollution are found, ORSANCO finds out where the pollution is coming from and makes sure it stops. When the river is high, ORSANCO also warns people where flooding may occur.

Right: *Orange chemicals are pumped into the river from a mine.*

warmer than most other furs because they have two layers. The outer layer prevents the animal from getting too cold by keeping the water away from the animal's skins.

River Fish

The Ohio River is home to more than 150 species of fish, including trout, carp, catfish, walleye, and bass. Although there is no large-scale fishing on the river, many amateur fishers catch and eat these fish. River authorities regularly collect fish from different parts of the river. They check to see whether or not the bodies of the fish contain pollutants. Pollutants from cities, farms, and mines get into the river in various ways.

Above: *A student tests Ohio River water using a machine that uses light to detect pollution.*

3 A Route to the West

Control of the Ohio River was fought over for many years. The winner would receive a land filled with opportunities and a river that offered the best means of traveling to the lands of the West.

People lived beside the Ohio River twelve thousand years ago, although historians know very little about them. The Adena were an ancient people that did leave their mark in the area, however. The Adena built large mounds of earth and stones along the Ohio. Some of these huge mounds are more than 2,500 years old. A few of the mounds were built to mark sacred places. Others cover the graves of important Native leaders. People studying the mounds have discovered log tombs

Below: *Great Serpent Mound at Hillsboro, Ohio, was built by Adena people hundreds of years ago. The mound is one-quarter of a mile (0.4 km) long.*

inside many of them. The tombs often contain gifts, such as pipes, for the dead buried there.

One of the largest burial mounds built by the Adena is Grave Creek Mound, which is beside the Ohio River at Moundsville, West Virginia. This huge mound is more than five stories high.

The Adena lived in small villages and survived by gathering wild plants, hunting, and fishing. They were skilled craft workers, making pots and jewelry. They traded these products to the Hopewell and other Native peoples in the area who also built mounds.

Newcomers

For thousands of years, the mound builders of the Ohio Valley lived peacefully. In the early seventeenth century, however, European pioneers came to the area to trade with Native people for the fur of forest animals. The fur was shipped back to Europe to make clothes.

The Iroquois invaded the Ohio Valley in the 1620s. The Iroquois Confederacy was an alliance of five Native groups (later six groups), mainly from the New York and New England areas. The confederacy brought modern guns and other weapons and used

them to take control of land from the Ohio River and Great Lakes to Maine.

The Iroquois sold furs to Europeans and controlled trade in the area. The Miami Confederacy was another alliance of Native people. This confederacy came from west of the Great Lakes. They battled with the Iroquois for control of the Ohio River fur trade during the seventeenth century. These conflicts were called the Beaver Wars.

LA CACCIA DEI CASTORI

Above: *An engraving made about 1750 shows Native people killing beavers in a tributary of the Ohio River. The beaver pelts were traded for guns and tools.*

European countries, mainly France and Britain, wanted to control the Ohio Valley themselves, however. In addition to the fur trade, they also wanted to use the Ohio River as a way of traveling west toward the Mississippi River and the vast prairies beyond.

European Powers

In 1669, French aristocrat Rene-Robert Cavelier de la Salle claimed the river and all the land around it for France. He called the Ohio the Beautiful River. Over the next ninety years, the British and French fought for the land. Each side befriended various Native groups in order to gain support in their fight. The British generally allied with the Iroquois, and the French were helped by the Miami. These years of fighting for the Ohio Valley were just part of a larger struggle between France and Britain for control of the whole of North America.

The struggle eventually became the French and Indian War (1756–1763). The first battle in this struggle took place in 1754 at the head of the Ohio River, close to where Pittsburgh stands today. The year before, the Iroquois had allowed a group of traders from

Virginia (which belonged to Britain at the time) to build roads and trading posts beside the Ohio River. The French government was worried that the British would take over all the land around the river. French soldiers destroyed the new settlements and built a fort at the head of the river.

Above: *French soldiers and Native warriors attack the British during a battle near present-day Pittsburgh.*

River Battles

George Washington, the future U.S. president, was a young Virginian soldier working for the British at this time. He was sent to remove the French from their fort. His army was easily defeated, however, and Washington was forced to surrender. He and his soldiers were released by the French and were fortunate to survive.

The fighting soon spread across North America and Europe, as Britain and France battled for control of territory around the world. Battles were also fought in India. After several attempts, the British eventually forced the French from their fort on the Ohio River in 1758.

The French and Indian War carried on elsewhere in North America until 1763, when France gave up. The British took control of most of eastern North America, from Canada to Florida.

CORNSTALK

Cornstalk was a Shawnee leader who led his people against Virginian settlers in a battle beside the Ohio River. The Shawnee people had moved to the Ohio Valley in the early part of the sixteenth century. By 1774, their land was being taken over by Virginians settling in the area, and Cornstalk feared that the whole of the Shawnee Nation would be taken away.

He raised an army and battled the settlers at Point Pleasant on the Ohio River. His army was defeated. In 1777, Cornstalk was visiting Point Pleasant when a settler was killed by a group of Native people. In revenge, a mob of Virginians murdered Cornstalk. After his death, the Shawnee moved west of the Mississippi. Today, most Shawnee people live in Oklahoma.

Pioneer Town

The British army built their own fort at the head of the Ohio River. They named it Fort Pitt for William Pitt, the British prime minister at the time. Over the next one hundred years, thousands of American and European pioneers traveled down the Ohio River in search of new ways of life to the west. Most traveled past Fort Pitt, and a town called Pittsburgh began to grow around the military outpost.

Early on, Pittsburgh's main industry was boatbuilding. Pioneers traveled overland to Pittsburgh. They then built rafts or bought boats to continue their journey by water. The boats were flat-bottomed so they would not run aground in shallow water. These boats were steered with oars or poles.

Many settlers chose to live in the new ports, such as Louisville and Cincinnati, that were developing beside the river. Others traveled inland from the riverbank, looking for land to turn into farms. They often followed trails, created by herds of wild buffalo, through the forest. Once the settlers

Below: *A hand-drawn panorama of Louisville, Kentucky, from 1876. By this time, more than 100,000 people lived in the city.*

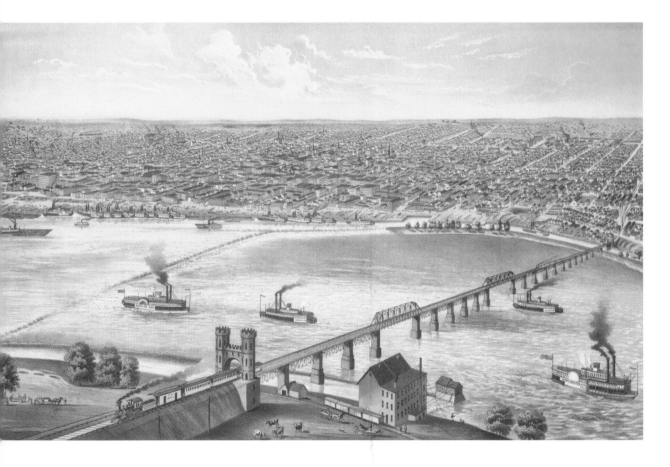

FIGHTING FOR THE OHIO RIVER

George Washington was involved in the battle for control of the Ohio River from an early stage. A Virginian soldier under the command of the British army, Washington realized that the Ohio River would be the best way for pioneers to travel to the west, and he urged the British to keep control of the river away from the French.

Washington's brothers, Lawrence and Augustine, were among a group of traders that began building settlements along the Ohio in the 1750s. Washington and his troops were on their way to defend the settlements when the first battles that became the French and Indian War started. The war made Washington one of the most famous soldiers in America.

reached their new homes, they broke up their rafts or boats and used the wood to build houses.

U.S. Territory

The number of settlers on the Ohio River increased after the founding of the United States. In 1786, a group of businesspeople from Virginia asked the U.S. Congress to lay claim to the land beyond the Ohio River. They called this land the Northwest Territory. The states of Ohio, Wisconsin, Minnesota, Indiana, Illinois, and Michigan make up this region today. By 1788, the first town in the new territory had been built where the Muskingum River flowed into the Ohio. The town was named Marietta, for Marie Antoinette, the Queen of France at the time.

Throughout the nineteenth century, the Ohio River

Above: *George Washington in the uniform of the colonial militia of Virginia.*

Above: *Near Pittsburgh in 1959, a plant extracting chemicals from coal puffs out smoke beside the Ohio River.*

became quite busy. As well as bringing new arrivals to the area, barges carried the products of the river's first industries. Near the river in Kentucky, salt licks—natural outcrops of rock salt—were dug up and turned into table salt. Coal from the eastern part of the Ohio Valley also became a common cargo on the river. Railroads were built to connect the river ports with other large towns, and the Ohio's banks were crowded with factories. In the 1870s, a new wave of immigrants came to the area from Europe. By the middle of the twentieth century, the Ohio River's cities were busy industrial centers.

BUILDING BRIDGES

Ambridge is a small town beside the Ohio River in Pennsylvania, a few miles downstream from Pittsburgh. The whole town was built in 1903 by the American Bridge Company, which needed a place for its workers to live. Ambridge was named for the company, and the residents worked in the town's factories, making the steel sections for large river barges and bridges. The town was so successful that, by 1930, twenty thousand people lived there. Most of these people were born outside of the United States. In 1926, the company built a bridge across the Ohio River to Aliquippa, where the large Jones & Laughlin steelworks was based. From then on, the two companies worked in partnership.

The people of Ambridge made the steel sections used in San Francisco's Oakland Bay Bridge and New York's Verrazano Narrows Bridge, which at the time was the largest in the world. They also made girders used to build the Chrysler Building and Empire State Building in New York and the Sears Tower in Chicago. In 1983, the American Bridge Company closed its factories in Ambridge, and the town is now a suburb of Pittsburgh.

Left: *Children play in the streets of Ambridge in 1938. Their fathers probably worked for the American Bridge Company.*

4 Center of Industry

The Ohio River is a busy stretch of water. Every year, huge river barges carry millions of tons of cargo from the mines, farms, and factories along the Ohio River to ports around the country.

The first settlers to travel down the Ohio River used simple rafts and boats. They floated with the river's current, which flowed east to west. Traveling up the river against the current was much harder. This changed when the Ohio's first steamboat was launched in 1811. Steamboats made the journey downriver quicker, and they could get back upstream using steam power.

Above: *A tug pushes fifteen barges out of the lock at Belleville Dam on the Ohio River near Parkersburg.*

Soon there were hundreds of steamboats on the river. This new way of traveling was good for business. The boats carried cargo and passengers to new river ports, such as Cincinnati, Louisville, and Huntington, which grew up rapidly.

Taming the River

Navigating safely around the sandbars and rapids was a difficult job, however. Many steamboats were wrecked and their valuable cargoes lost. Also, in the early nineteenth century, boats could not travel past Louisville toward the Mississippi River because they were blocked by the treacherous waters of the Falls of the Ohio at that point. Traders demanded

KENTUCKY DERBY

The Kentucky Derby is probably the most famous horse race in the United States. It takes place on the first Saturday of May at Churchill Downs racetrack. This track is in Louisville, Kentucky, just a few miles from the Ohio River.

In this race, three-year-old horses run 1.25 miles (2 km). This race has been held every year since 1875, making it the oldest race in the United States. A museum at the racetrack tells the story of this world-famous sporting event.

Racers in the Kentucky Derby pass underneath the famous towers at Churchill Downs.

STEEL PRODUCTION

Iron and steel production is an important part of the Ohio Valley's economy. Many of the region's steelworks are based along the shore of Lake Erie, to the north of the Ohio River. Pittsburgh alone, at the head of the river, produces about one-fifth of the United States' steel.

Iron metal is extracted from rock called iron ore. Coal and limestone are used in this process. All three of these natural materials are found in or near the Ohio Valley, although most of the iron ore comes from Canada. Some ore is shipped along the Mississippi River and then up the Ohio River.

Coal is shipped from West Virginia down the Monongahela River to the steelworks. Limestone is mined in Kentucky and carried up the Ohio River to Pittsburgh. The steel is used to make machinery or automobile parts in riverside factories.

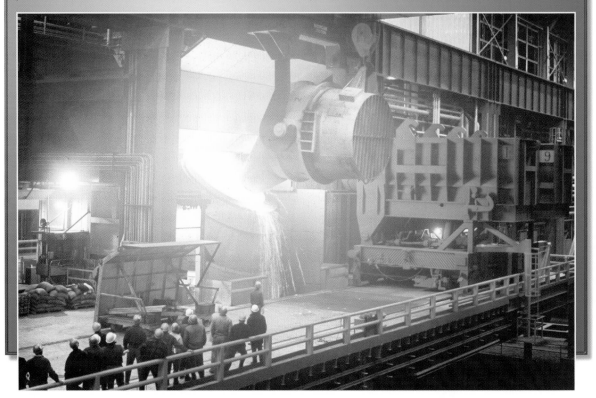

Above: *Liquid iron is poured into a blast furnace, where it is turned into steel. Steel is a mixture of iron and carbon and is much tougher than pure iron.*

that Congress do something to make the river safer. In 1824, the U.S. Army Corps of Engineers began removing such hazards as rocks and sandbanks from the river. This made journeys safer, but the water was too shallow in many places for large boats to pass. In 1830, a canal was dug around the Falls of the Ohio, making the river open to traffic along its entire length.

Locks and Dams
In 1878, the U.S. Army returned to build a lock and dam at Davis Island, a few miles downriver from the

Left: *A tugboat pushes twenty-five coal barges along the Ohio River. The coal is being taken to a power plant.*

city of Pittsburgh. Once completed, this lock was the largest in the world at the time. The lock gates were opened when the river was filled with plenty of water. When the river's level began to drop, the lock was closed. This kept the water behind the dam deep enough for boats to travel safely.

By 1929, the Ohio had fifty-three dams along its course. Before the last dam was finished, however, the older ones upstream were being replaced with more modern designs. Today, the river has just twenty dams, which always keep the river at least 9 feet (2.7 m) deep. The dams are also part of the river's flood defenses.

The Ohio floods in spring, as winter snow melts on the mountain slopes and flows into the Ohio through its tributaries. Surges of water are controlled by the dams so the river does not flood riverside towns.

The Ohio River's dams are also an important source of energy. The dams' forty-nine power plants produce 6 percent of the all the power used in the United States.

Above: *A river barge at the entrance to a canal that provides a route around the Falls of the Ohio at Louisville.*

River Transportation

Twenty-five million people —that is almost one in ten U.S. residents—live in the Ohio River area. Even though river transportation is not as important to the region today as it was in the past, the Ohio is still busy. In the United States, only the Mississippi River carries more cargo than the Ohio. Over 230 million tons (209 million tonnes) of cargo are carried on barges up and down the river each year. Because the Ohio flows into the Mississippi, products made in Pittsburgh and other cities along the river can travel all the way to the Gulf of Mexico and from there to the rest of the world.

Below: *A view of downtown Cincinnati from Kentucky, across the Ohio River.*

CINCINNATI: PORT OF PATRIOTS

Cincinnati, Ohio, is one of the largest cities and most important ports on the Ohio River. It lies on the north bank of the river across from Covington, Kentucky. The bridge that connects the two ports was built by the same team of engineers that later erected the Brooklyn Bridge, which spans the East River in New York City.

In 1790, General Arthur St. Clair changed the name of Losantiville, a tiny riverside village, to Cincinnati. He took the name from a society of soldiers, who followed the example of Cincinnatus, a great Roman patriot.

As Cincinnati grew rich with river trade, people came from all over the world, but mainly from Germany and Ireland, to make their homes in the city. By the late nineteenth century, Cincinnati was the largest producer of processed meat products in the country. Live animals were shipped to the city, and the meat processed there was shipped out, also by way of the river. Today, 46 million tons (42 million tonnes) of cargo pass through the port every year.

The railroad came to Cincinnati in the 1870s, joining the port with cities to the south. Since that time, the city has become a center of manufacturing. Procter & Gamble, the soap company, has factories there, making Cincinnati the largest producer of soap in the world. The city also produces aircraft engines, chemicals, and aluminum.

Nearly three-quarters of all the cargo carried on the Ohio River is coal. Coal is mined in several places in the region. To the east, in Pennsylvania and West Virginia, mines produce anthracite. Anthracite is a type of coal that is hard and burns hotter than any other type of coal. The coal mines farther west, in Ohio and Kentucky, produce softer coals that are not as valuable as anthracite. Natural gas and oil are also found in Ohio and Indiana.

Rock On

The states of Ohio and Kentucky are important sources of limestone and sandstone. Limestone is used in iron production and the chemical industry. It is also used to make glass, another important industry in those states.

Sandstone is used in bricks, tiles, and other building materials. More than one-third of the United States' sandstone comes from the Ohio River region.

All these raw materials have made the Ohio Valley a manufacturing center. The metals produced in the area are used to make parts for automobiles and machinery.

In addition, farmers grow soybeans and corn and raise hogs and cattle. Many of these foods are packaged in riverside factories, before being shipped out.

Above: *Stone is dug out of a quarry beside the Ohio River near Cairo, Illinois, before being loaded onto barges.*

5 Places to Visit

Many places of natural beauty and historic interest, as well as some of the most important industrial and historic cities in the United States, line the Ohio River.

❶ Allegheny National Forest, Pennsylvania

The Allegheny River, one of the tributaries of the Ohio River, flows through this beautiful area. People come to hike and camp or to boat on the mountain lakes

❷ The Point, Pittsburgh

This triangular point marks the head of the Ohio River, at the heart of the city of Pittsburgh. The very tip of the point is covered by Point Start Park, while the rest makes up the downtown district.

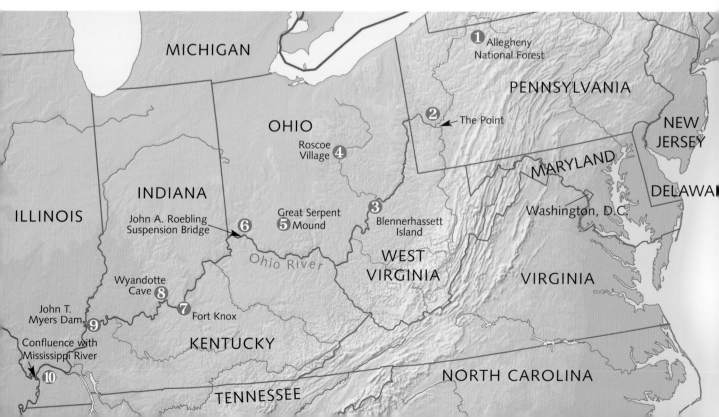

3 Blennerhassett Island, West Virginia

This island in the Ohio River gets its name from Harman Blennerhassett, a wealthy British aristocrat, who built a magnificent mansion on the island in 1798.

4 Roscoe Village, Ohio

A restored 1830s settlement that brings the Ohio River and Erie Canal to life. This canal was once the main route between the Ohio River and the Great Lakes. The village has historic homes and businesses, as well as a horse-drawn canal boat.

5 Great Serpent Mound, Hillsboro, Ohio

Perhaps the most spectacular of the mounds made by the Adena people, this nine-hundred-year-old burial mound is shaped like a serpent and is a quarter of a mile (0.4 km) long.

7 Fort Knox, Kentucky

This world-famous fort houses more than six billion dollars worth of the U.S. Treasury Department's gold. During World War II (1939–1945), the supersecure depository kept the U.S. Constitution, the Declaration of Independence, the Gutenberg Bible, Lincoln's Gettysburg Address, and the Magna Carta safe.

6

6 John A. Roebling Suspension Bridge, Covington, Kentucky

This bridge connects Covington to Cincinnati, Ohio. It was named after the man who built it in 1866. He later built the Brooklyn Bridge.

8 Wyandotte Cave, Indiana

This is one of the largest caverns in the United States. It has five levels, 35 miles (56 km) of underground passages, and many large chambers.

9 John T. Myers Locks and Dam, Uniontown, Kentucky

This structure crosses the Ohio a few miles (km) from the mouth of the river. It is 3,504 feet (1,068 m) wide. The dam is positioned a few miles upstream from where the Wabash River flows into the Ohio.

10 Confluence with the Mississippi River in Cairo, Illinois

At Cairo, the Ohio flows into the Mississippi. At this point, the Ohio carries more water than the Mississippi, but the Mississippi carries more as it flows to the sea.

How Rivers Form

Rivers have many features that are constantly changing in shape. The illustration below shows how these features are created.

Rivers flow from mountains to oceans, receiving water from rain, melting snow, and underground springs. Rivers collect their water from an area called the river basin. High mountain ridges form the divides between river basins.

Tributaries join the main river at places called confluences. Rivers flow down steep mountain slopes quickly but slow as they near the ocean and gather more water. Slow rivers have many meanders (wide turns) and often change course.

Near the mouth, levees (piles of mud) build up on the banks. The levees stop water from draining into the river, creating areas of swamp.

❶ **Glacier:** An ice mass that melts into river water.

❷ **Lake:** The source of many rivers; may be fed by springs or precipitation.

❸ **Rapids:** Shallow water that flows quickly.

❹ **Waterfall:** Formed when a river wears away softer rock, making a step in the riverbed.

❺ **Canyon:** Formed when a river cuts a channel through rock.

❻ **Floodplain:** A place where rivers often flood flat areas, depositing mud.

❼ **Oxbow lake:** River bend cut off when a river changes course, leaving water behind.

❽ **Estuary:** River mouth where river and ocean water mix together.

❾ **Delta:** Triangular river mouth created when mud islands form, splitting the flow into several channels called distributaries.

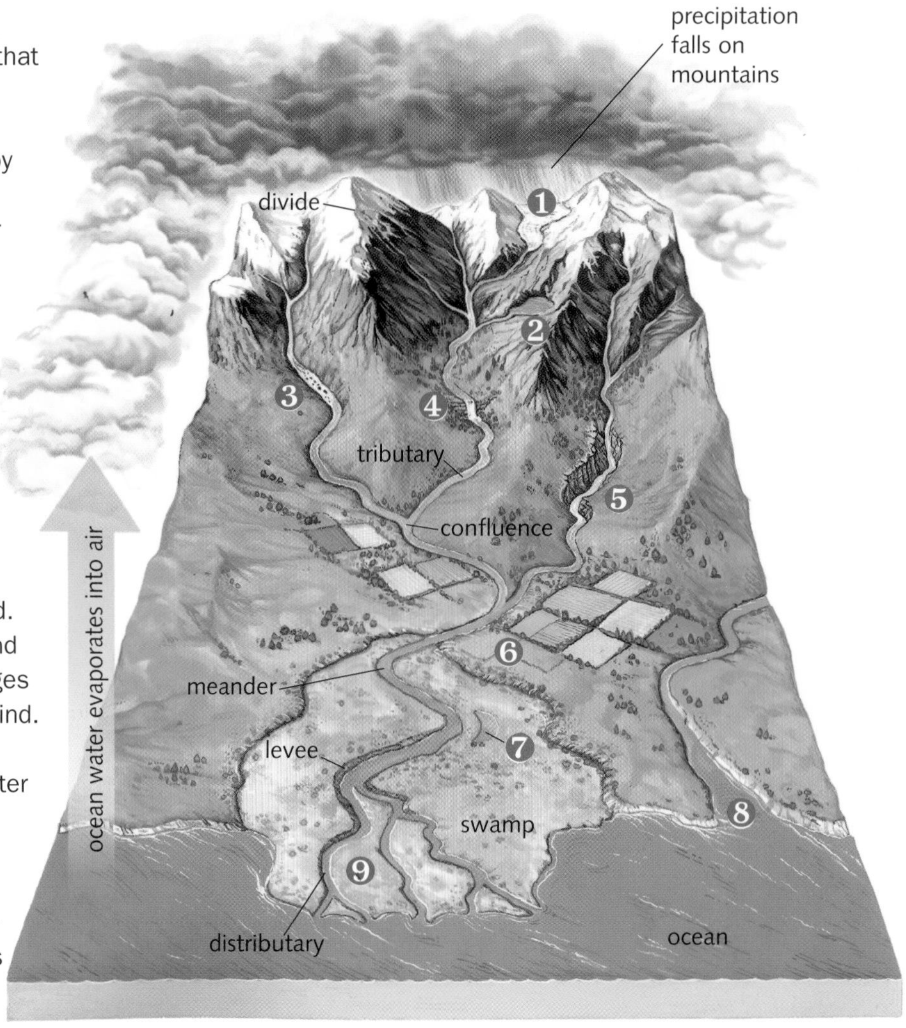

precipitation falls on mountains

divide

tributary

confluence

meander

levee

swamp

distributary

ocean

ocean water evaporates into air

Glossary

barge A flat-bottomed boat used to transport goods and usually pulled or pushed by a tug.

basin The area drained by a river and its tributaries.

confederacy People united in a league to support common interests.

confluence The place where rivers meet.

dam A constructed barrier across a river that controls the flow of water.

depository A place where valuable things are kept locked up for safety.

flatboat A flat-bottomed barge that can travel through shallow water.

industry Producing things or providing services in order to earn money.

lock A section of a river that is enclosed by gates. The level of water inside the lock can be raised or lowered so boats can travel between stretches of water that are at different levels.

militia An army of volunteers who fight alongside regular army soldiers during emergencies. Each North American colony had its own militia.

navigate To travel through water, steering in an attempt to avoid obstacles.

ore Stone that contains metal or other valuable elements.

panorama An unbroken view of a wide area.

prairie Vast areas of grassland.

steel Iron metal mixed with a small amount of carbon and varying amounts of other metals to make it strong or hard wearing.

suspension bridge A bridge that is hung from cables attached to tall towers.

tributary A river that flows into a larger river at a confluence.

valley A hollow channel cut by a river, usually between ranges of hills or mountains.

For Further Information

Books

Eckert, Allan W. *That Dark and Bloody River: Chronicles of the Ohio River Valley.* Bantam Doubleday, 1996.

Hiscock, Bruce. *The Big Rivers: The Missouri, the Mississippi, and the Ohio.* Atheneum, 1997.

Ryle, Russell G. *Ohio River Images: Cincinnati to Louisville in the Packet Boat Era.* Arcadia, 2000.

Web Sites

First American West: The Ohio River Valley
memory.loc.gov/ammem/award99/icuhtml/fawhome.html

Grave Creek Mound Historic Site
www.wvculture.org/sites/gravecreek.html

Ohio River System
www.lrp.usace.army.mil/nav/ohioback.htm

Ohio River Valley Water Sanitation Commission
www.orsanco.org

Index